C000016491

SHAKES AND QUAKES

Natural Disasters that Change the Earth

Science Book 5th Grade | Children's Earth Sciences Books

First Edition, 2020

Published in the United States by Speedy Publishing LLC, 40 E Main Street, Newark, Delaware 19711 USA.

Baby Professor Books are available at special discounts when purchased in bulk for industrial and sales-promotional use. For details contact our Special Sales Team at Speedy Publishing LLC, 40 E Main Street, Newark, Delaware 19711 USA. Telephone (888) 248-4521 Fax: (210) 519-4043. www.speedybookstore.com

10 9 8 7 6 * 5 4 3 2 1

Print Edition: 9781541949430
Digital Edition: 9781541951235

See the world in pictures. Build your knowledge in style.
www.speedypublishing.com

TABLE OF CONTENTS

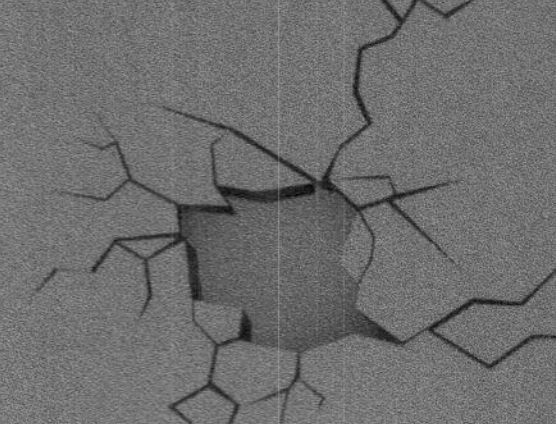

In this book, we're going to talk about earthquakes, so let's get right to it!

WHAT IS AN EARTHQUAKE?

The Earth's crust is always moving.

hen we stand outside in our backyards or inside our houses, we think of the ground under our feet as firm and solid, but this isn't really true. The reality is that the Earth's crust is always moving.

Molten rock surface

Massive layers of solid and molten rock are moving over and under each other. Sometimes we can feel the movement, but most of the time we can't.

If you live in an area where there's a sizable earthquake, you can feel the ground shaking. In fact, when there's a very powerful earthquake, you can actually feel the ground move in a wavelike motion under your feet just as if it were water.

A family taking cover under the table during an earthquake.

Most earthquakes only last a few seconds, but the most powerful earthquake ever recorded was the Valdivia earthquake, which took place in Chile in 1960 and could be felt for 10 minutes.

Valdivia after a 10-minute earthquake, 1960

Powerful earthquakes change the surface of the Earth. They can cause the ground to crack open and mounds of earth to push up and create cliffs.

Cracked asphalt road, aftermath of an earthquake

As the surface shakes, buildings are leveled and dams break.

A building destroyed by an earthquake

Volcanoes sometimes erupt as molten rock spews out of them and hits the Earth's surface.

Volcano Fuego in Antigua, Guatemala

Depending on where the center of the earthquake is, it may cause a tsunami as well. A tsunami is a gigantic sea wave that hits the shore and causes massive destruction.

A concept of a city destroyed by Tsunami waves

On average, a powerful quake happens yearly somewhere in the world. Every year earthquakes around the world are the cause of about 10,000 deaths.

Army clearing the city after the earthquake damage in Nepal

WHAT ARE TECTONIC PLATES?

16

For thousands of years, people had no clue what caused earthquakes. Ancient people thought that if they did something to make their gods angry that the gods would destroy them by making the ground below them shake!

An illustration of the destruction caused by an earthquake in Ancient Greece would have looked like.

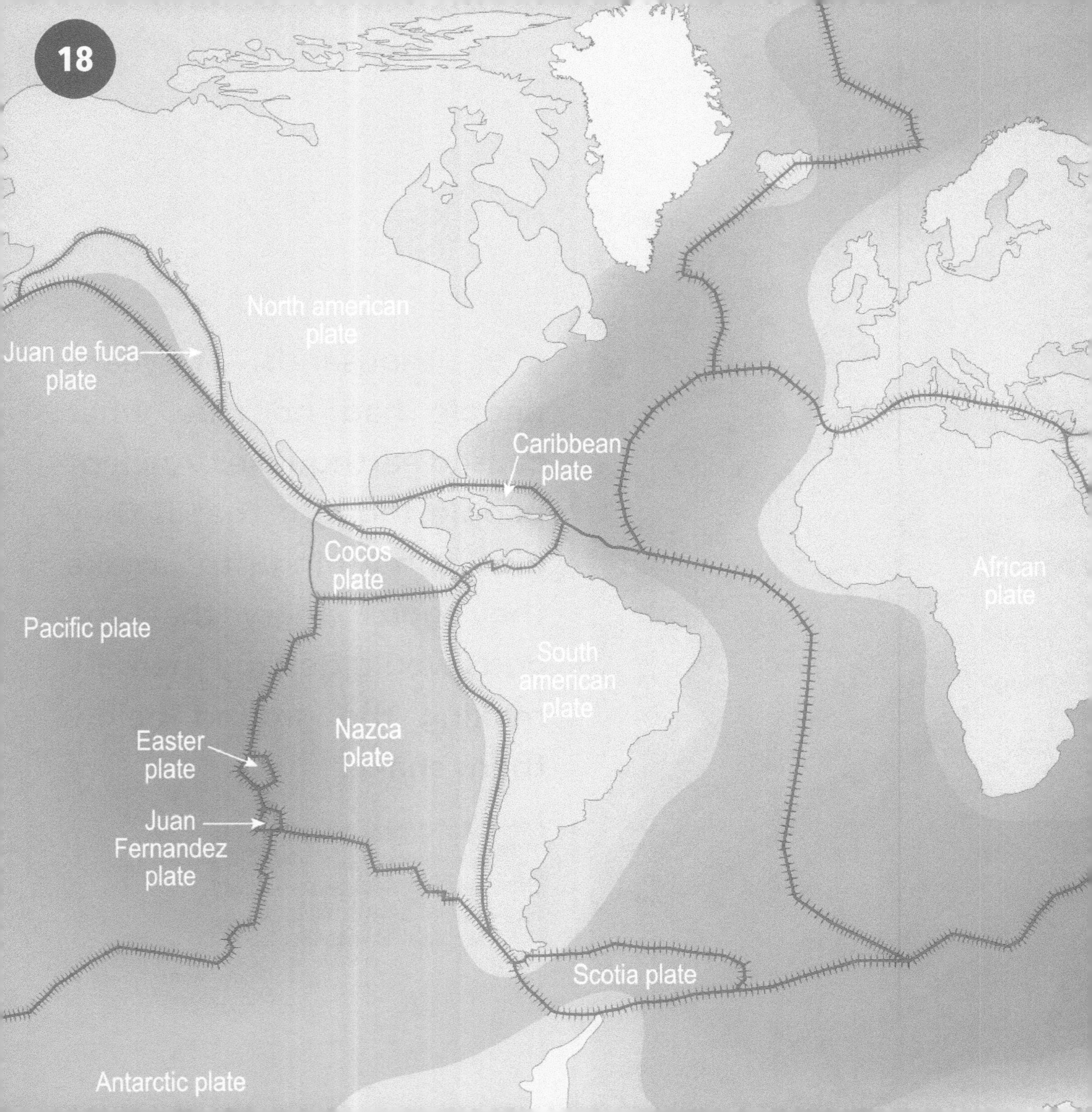
18
North american plate
Juan de fuca plate
Caribbean plate
Cocos plate
Pacific plate
African plate
South american plate
Nazca plate
Easter plate
Juan Fernandez plate
Scotia plate
Antarctic plate

It wasn't until 1910 when the plate tectonic theory was offered as a possible explanation for earthquakes. However, it wasn't until the 1950s that the theory was widely accepted.

PLATE TECTONICS

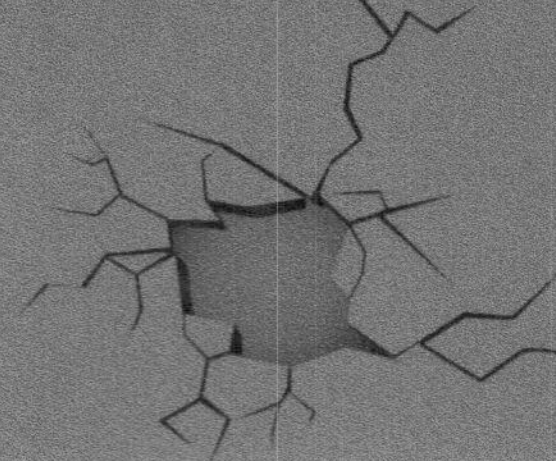

If you ever looked at the continents closely on a map or globe, you may have noticed that the continent of South America and the continent of Africa look like they might have fit together like puzzle pieces.

The continents of South America and Africa look like matching puzzle pieces.

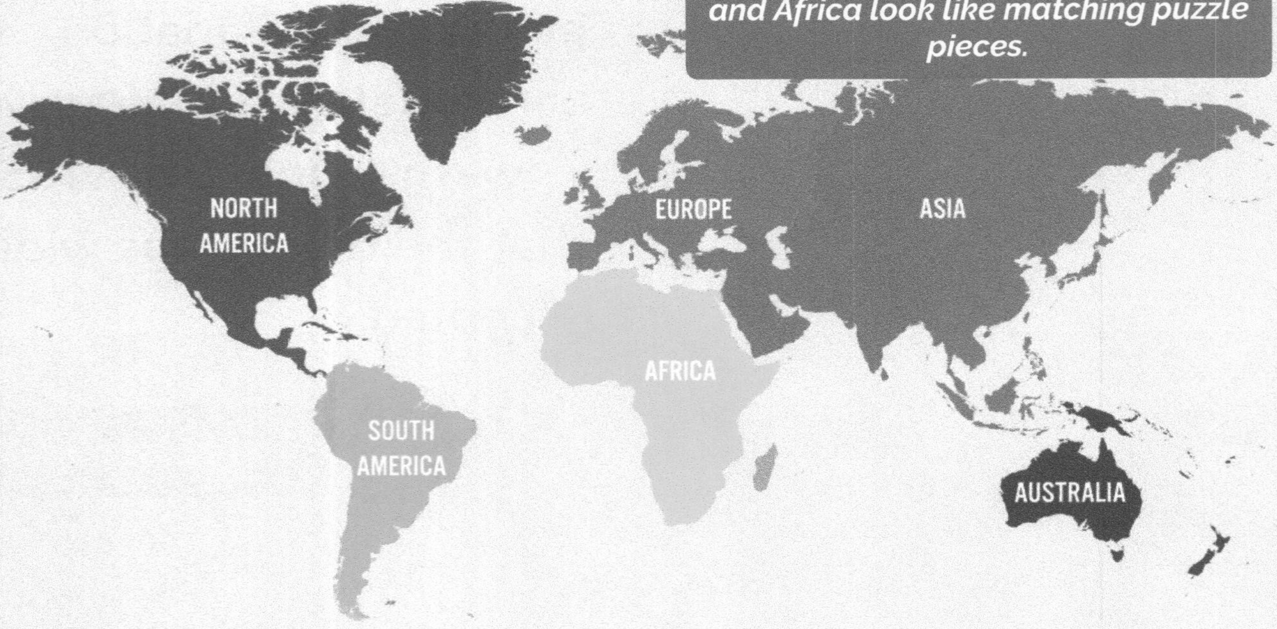

NORTH AMERICA
EUROPE
ASIA
AFRICA
SOUTH AMERICA
AUSTRALIA

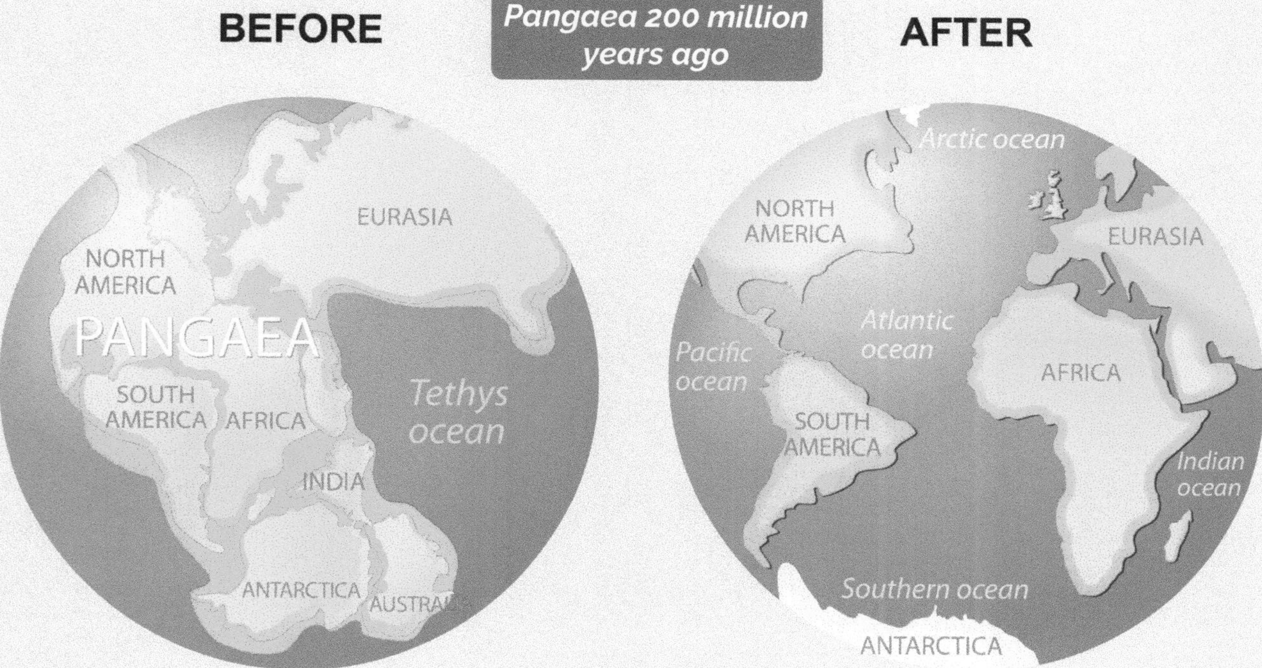

That's because all the continents that we have today were one gigantic landmass at one time. Scientists call this former massive continent, Pangaea. It existed 200 million years in the past.

Pangaea

Permian period
225 million years ago

Laurasia

Gondwana

Triassic period
200 million years ago

Jurassic period
150 million years ago

Cretaceous period
65 million years ago

The Continental drift

Millions of years from now, the continents won't be in the same position that they are today. The reason is that the tectonic plates keep shifting a few centimeters every year. Currently, North America and South America are moving toward Japan and the countries of Asia and away from Africa and Europe. This type of movement is called continental drift.

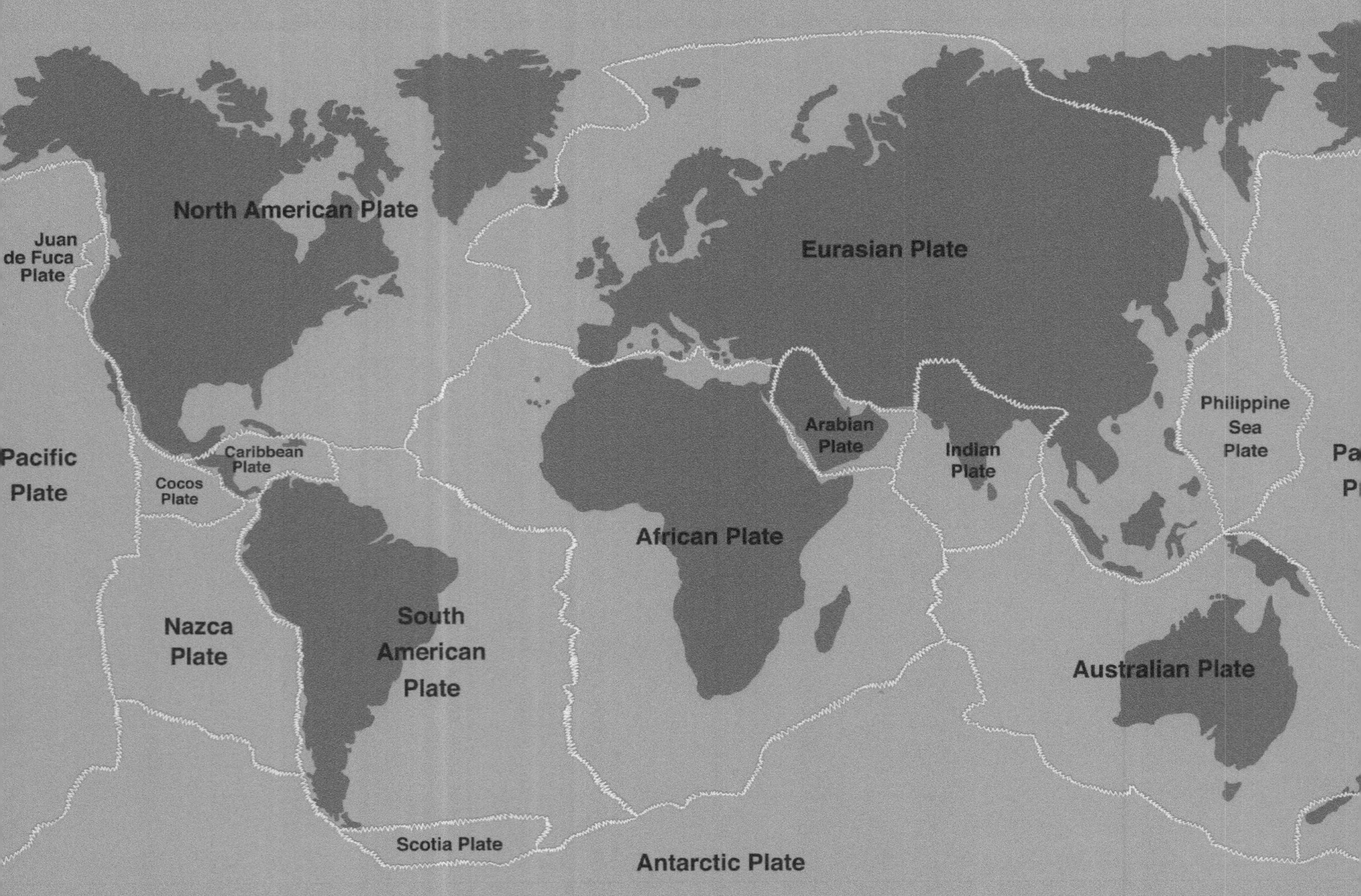

Tectonic plates with major and minor plates

When you hear the word "plate" you probably think of a dinner plate, but tectonic plates are enormous slabs of rock. If you look at a map with these tectonic plates marked, you would see that there are eight large plates that cover the Earth's surface as well as quite a few smaller plates.

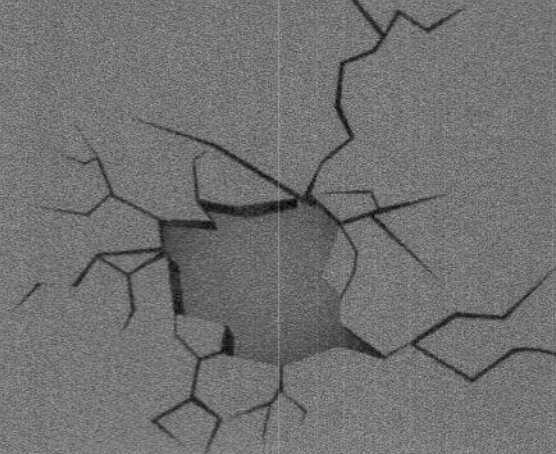

The lithosphere is the Earth's top layer that contains these tectonic plates. The tectonic plates carry areas of the continents as well as areas of the ocean. Think of these plates as if they were the planet's skin. Even though the plates are enormously heavy they actually float on top of the layer below them!

The lithosphere is the outer part of the Earth's crust where tectonic plates float on.

Plate Tectonics Theory

Mountain Range

High Plateau

Continental Crust

ntinental Crust

Lithosphere

Lithosphere

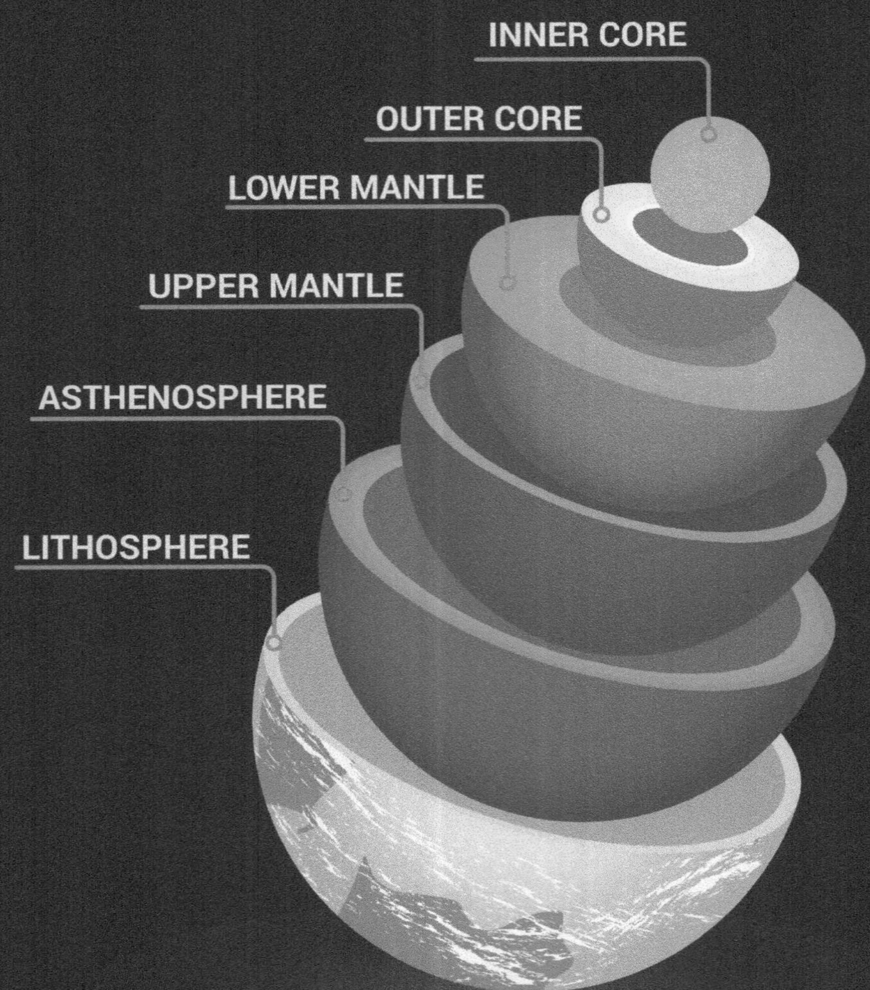

The layer that lies below them is called the asthenosphere. The asthenosphere is composed of magma, which is liquid rock. If you've ever seen pictures of how lava looks when it comes out of a volcano, then you know how magma looks.

The asthenosphere is composed of partially molten rock.

Scientists use the term "magma" for the liquid rock that's under the Earth's surface and the term "lava" for the same liquid rock that erupts from a volcano.

Lava from Nyiragongo Vulcan, Congo

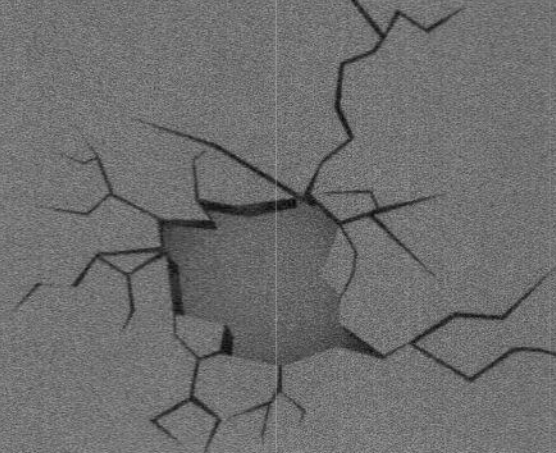

In addition to the way the continents fit together, there is another evidence that the theory of tectonic plates is correct as well. Scientists have discovered fossils that show that certain landmasses were connected in the past because they have the same animal and plant life.

Continental drift fossil evidence

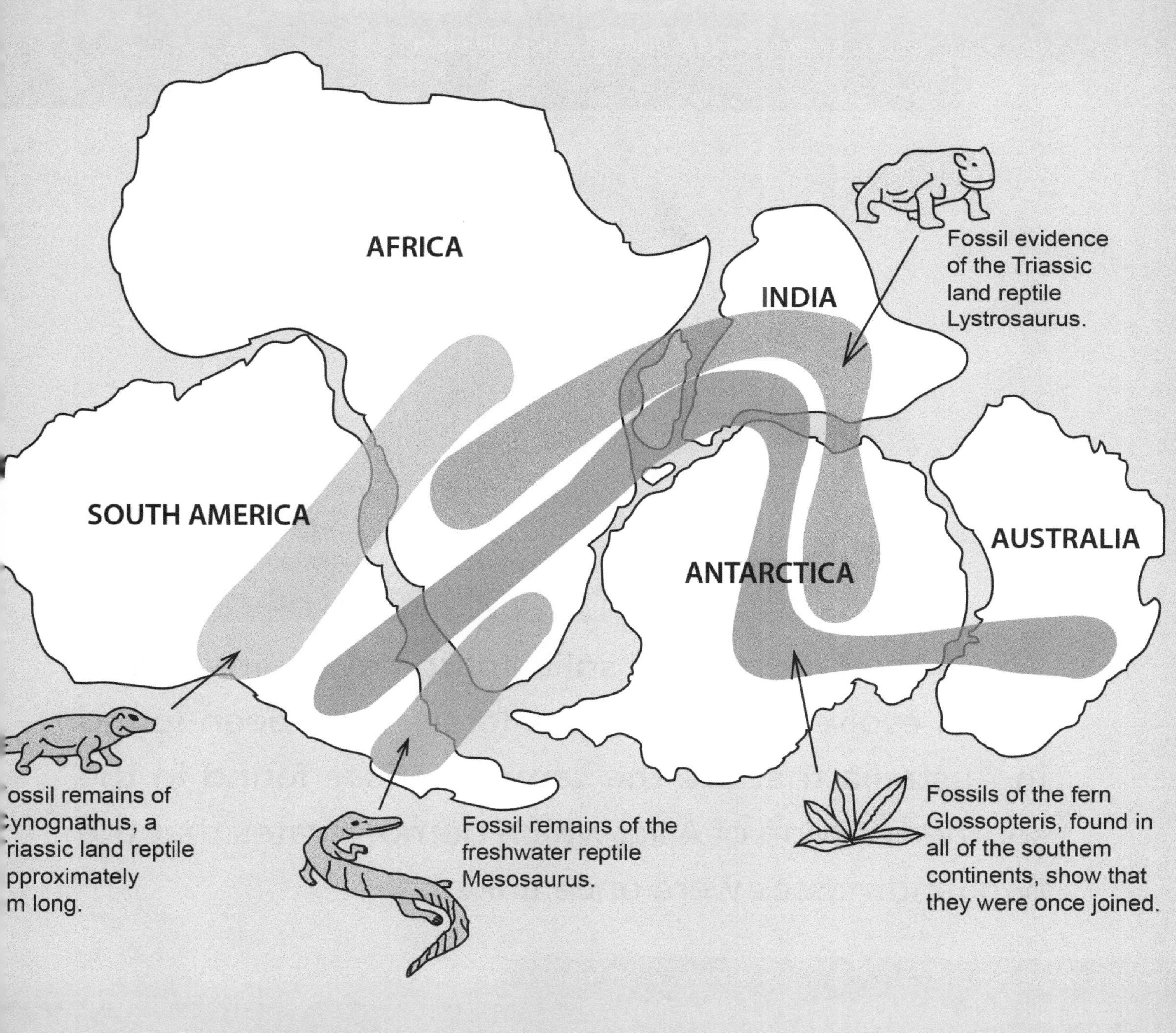
AFRICA
INDIA
Fossil evidence
of the Triassic
land reptile
Lystrosaurus.
SOUTH AMERICA
ANTARCTICA
AUSTRALIA
ossil remains of
ynognathus, a
riassic land reptile
pproximately
m long.
Fossil remains of the
freshwater reptile
Mesosaurus.
Fossils of the fern
Glossopteris, found in
all of the southern
continents, show that
they were once joined.

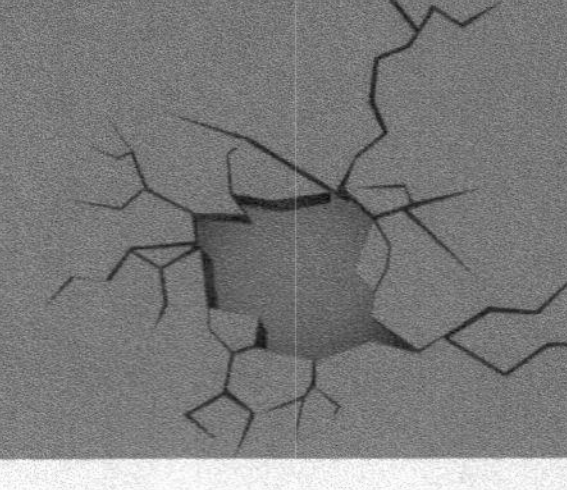

Fossils of Tetragraptus have been found in Australia, China and some other countries.

When the landmasses split apart, new animals and plants evolved. For example, fossils have been found in Australia that are the same as those found in the southern region of Asia, which demonstrates that the two landmasses were once linked.

One last point of evidence is that the rock formations sometimes match. For example, geologists compared the west coastline of Africa to the east coastline of South America where the two continents appear to match like puzzle pieces. The types of rock formations are so similar that it can't possibly be a coincidence.

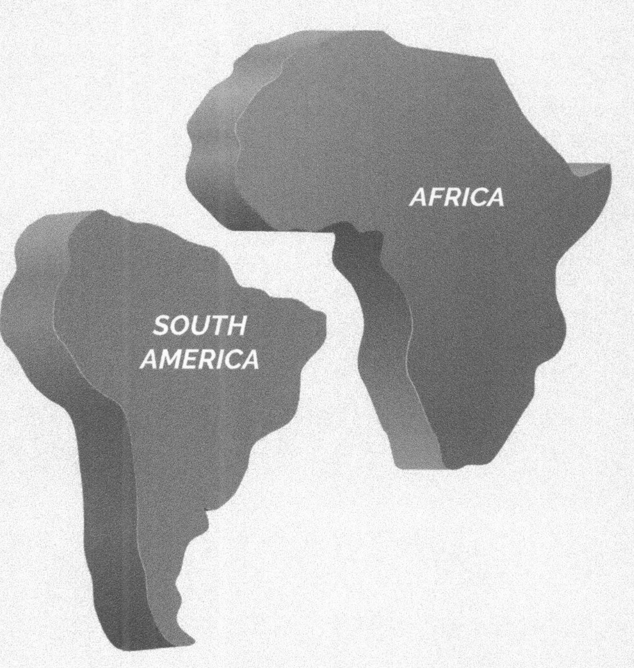

A 3d map of South America and Africa matching like puzzle pieces.

WHAT CAUSES EARTHQUAKES?

Underneath the continents, the Earth's crust is about 35 kilometers (22 miles) in thickness. However, the crust is not continuous.

An illustration of Earth's crust

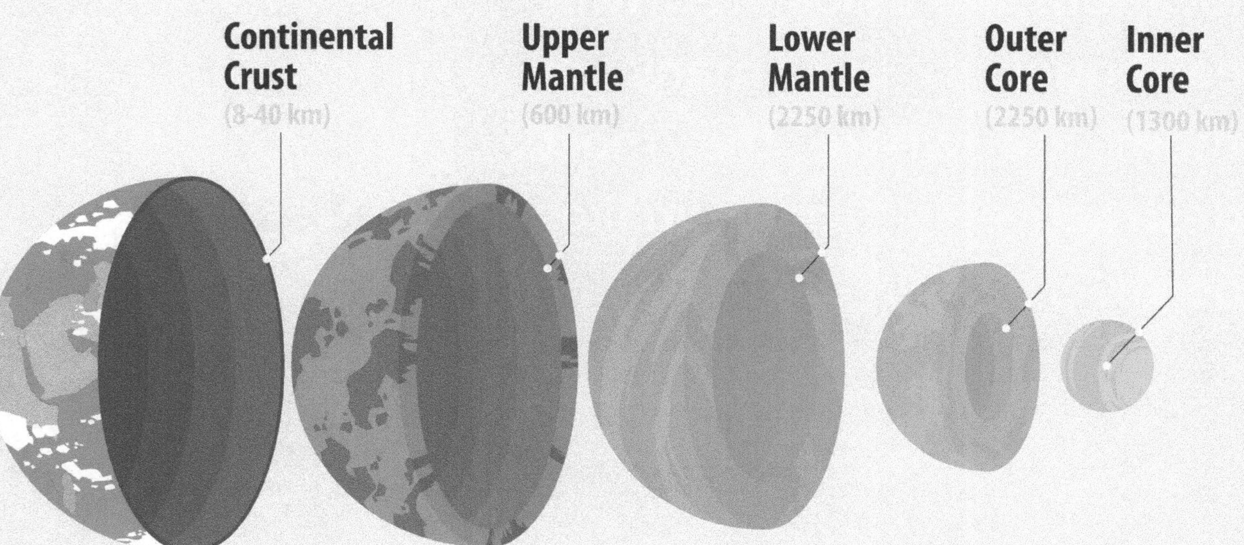

It is ruptured in places and those ruptures are called faults. Not all of these locations are associated with earthquakes, but many of them are where the most destructive earthquakes occur.

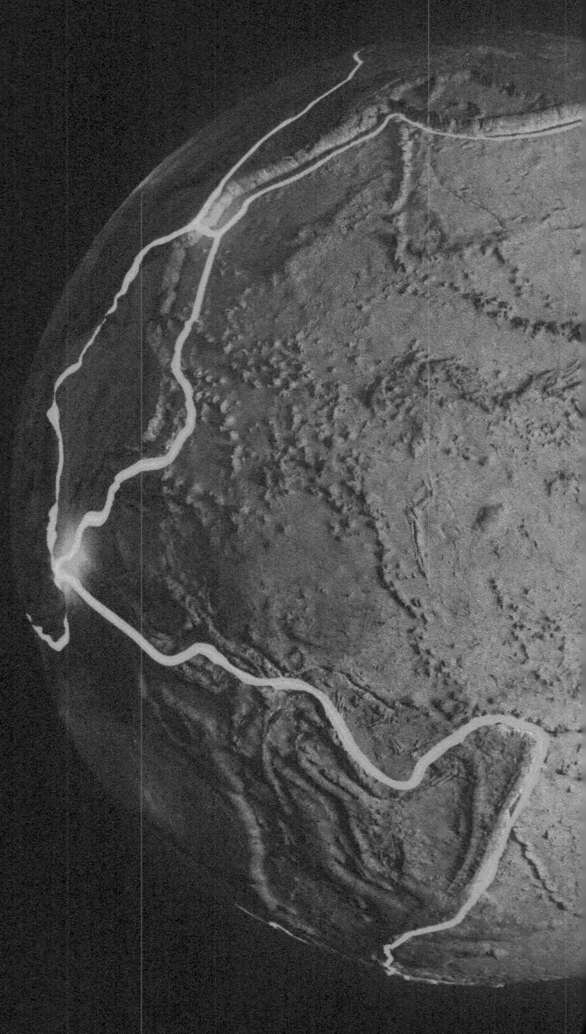

Earth's fault lines between tectonic plates

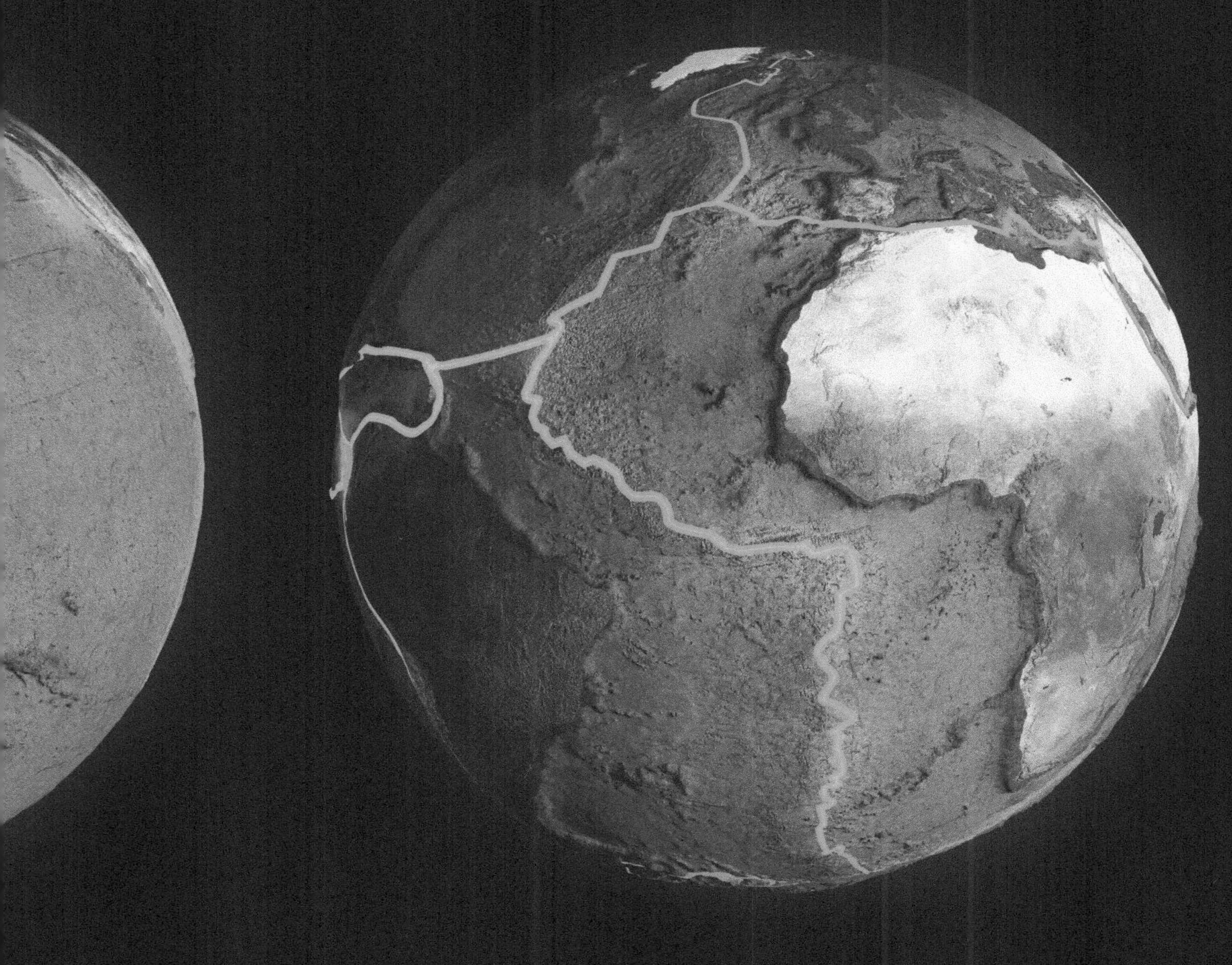

Earth's inner core is very hot.

The center of the Earth is very hot. The heat and radiation from the Earth's core is what melts the rock into flowing liquid magma. The pressure from the heat and the flowing magma builds up in the tectonic plates that compose the crust and then they start moving in relationship to each other along the faults.

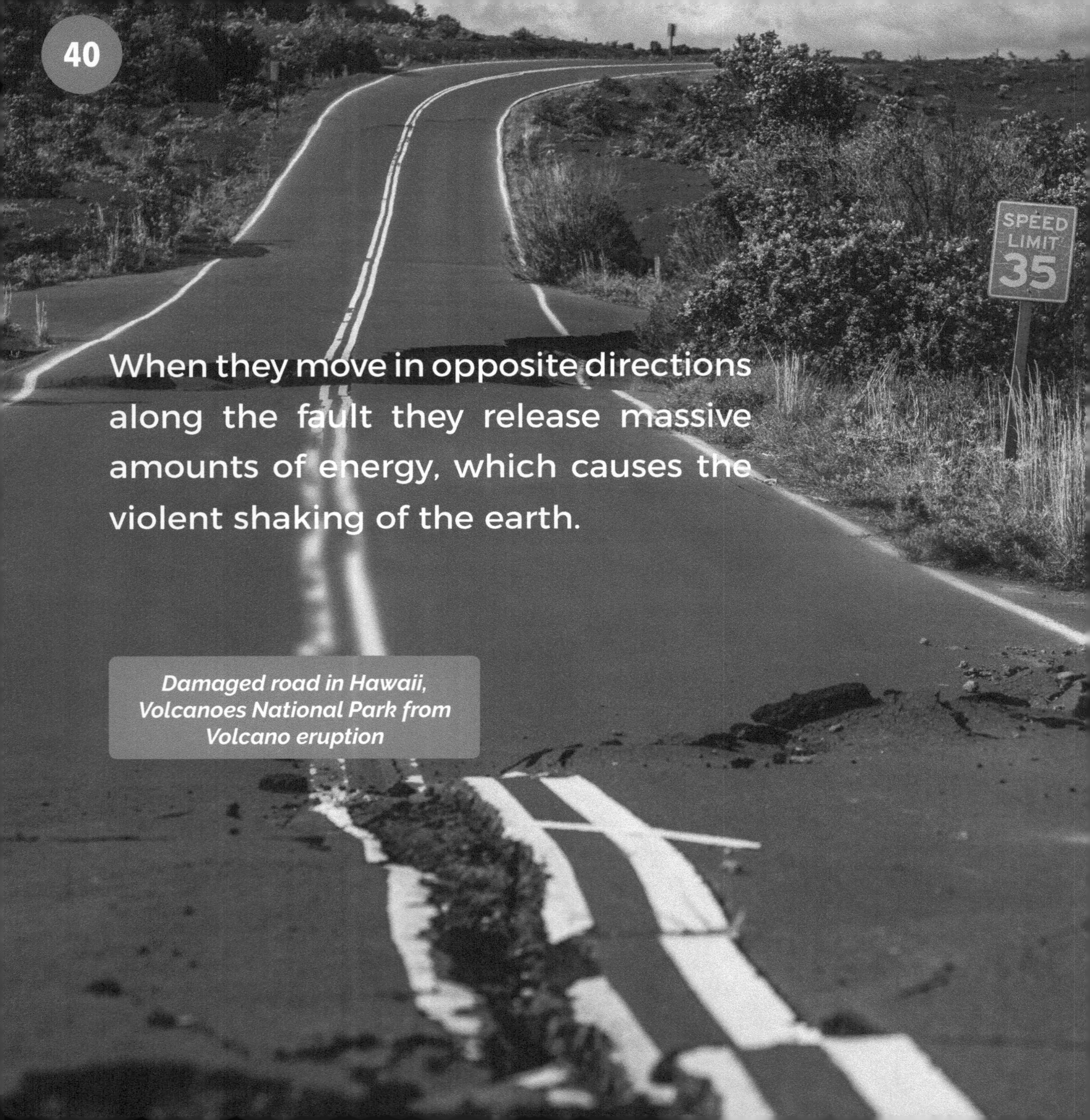

When they move in opposite directions along the fault they release massive amounts of energy, which causes the violent shaking of the earth.

Damaged road in Hawaii, Volcanoes National Park from Volcano eruption

There are many different ways they can move. When this happens, above ground, the displacement might be as little as a few centimeters to as much as many meters depending on the movements and the force.

Destroyed houses in Kathmandu, Nepal after the earthquake, April 2015

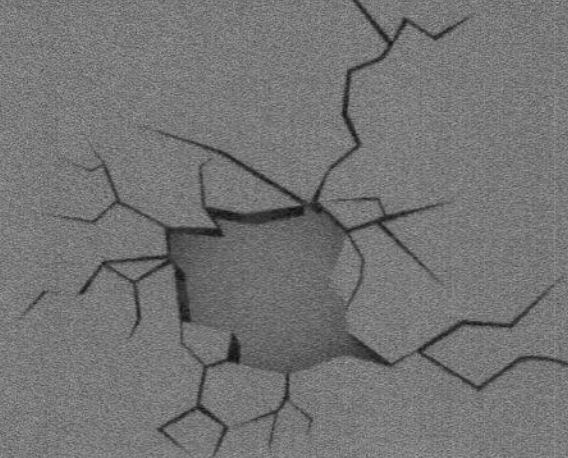

Seismologists, who are scientists that study earthquakes, have specific terminology for the movements of tectonic plates.

Plate Boundaries—the locations were plates meet and move

Convergent Boundary—a location where plates move toward one another...in other words, they converge

Divergent Boundary—a location where plates move opposite or away from one another...in other words, they diverge

Transform Boundary—a location where plates slide sideways past each other

THREE TYPES OF PLATE BOUNDARY

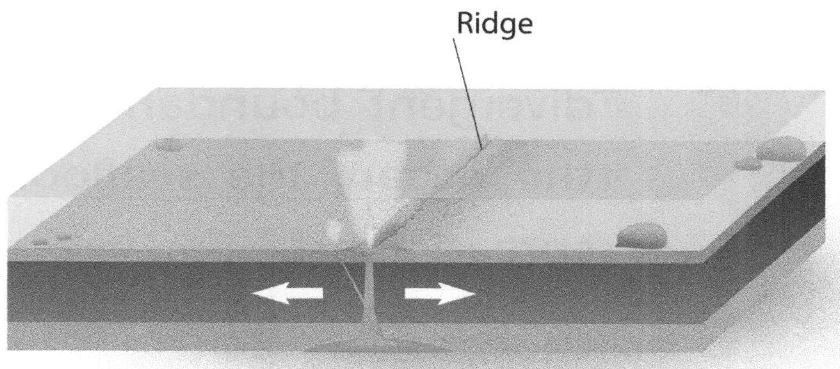

Transform plate boundary

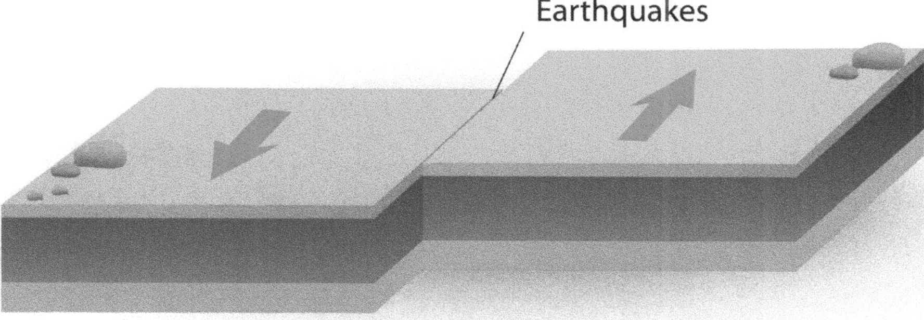

Convergent plate boundary

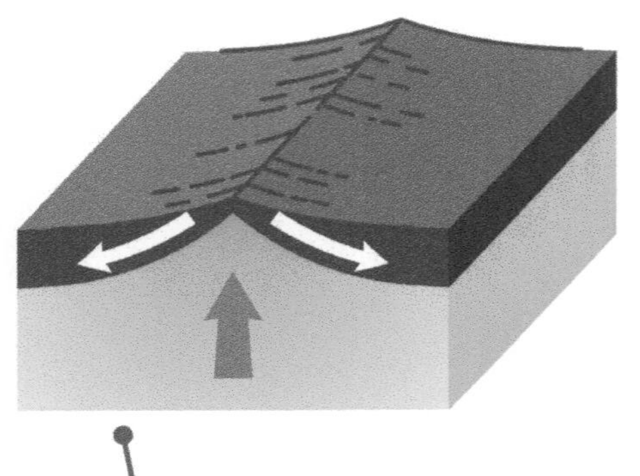

When plates move, it's not only continents that are affected, the oceans are affected as well. When divergent boundaries occur under the ocean, the seafloor begins to spread apart.

Divergent plate boundary in the ocean

Because of the movements of the continents, as North and South America are moving away from Europe and Africa, new seafloor is currently being created in the Atlantic Ocean.

North and South America are slowly moving away from Europe and Africa.

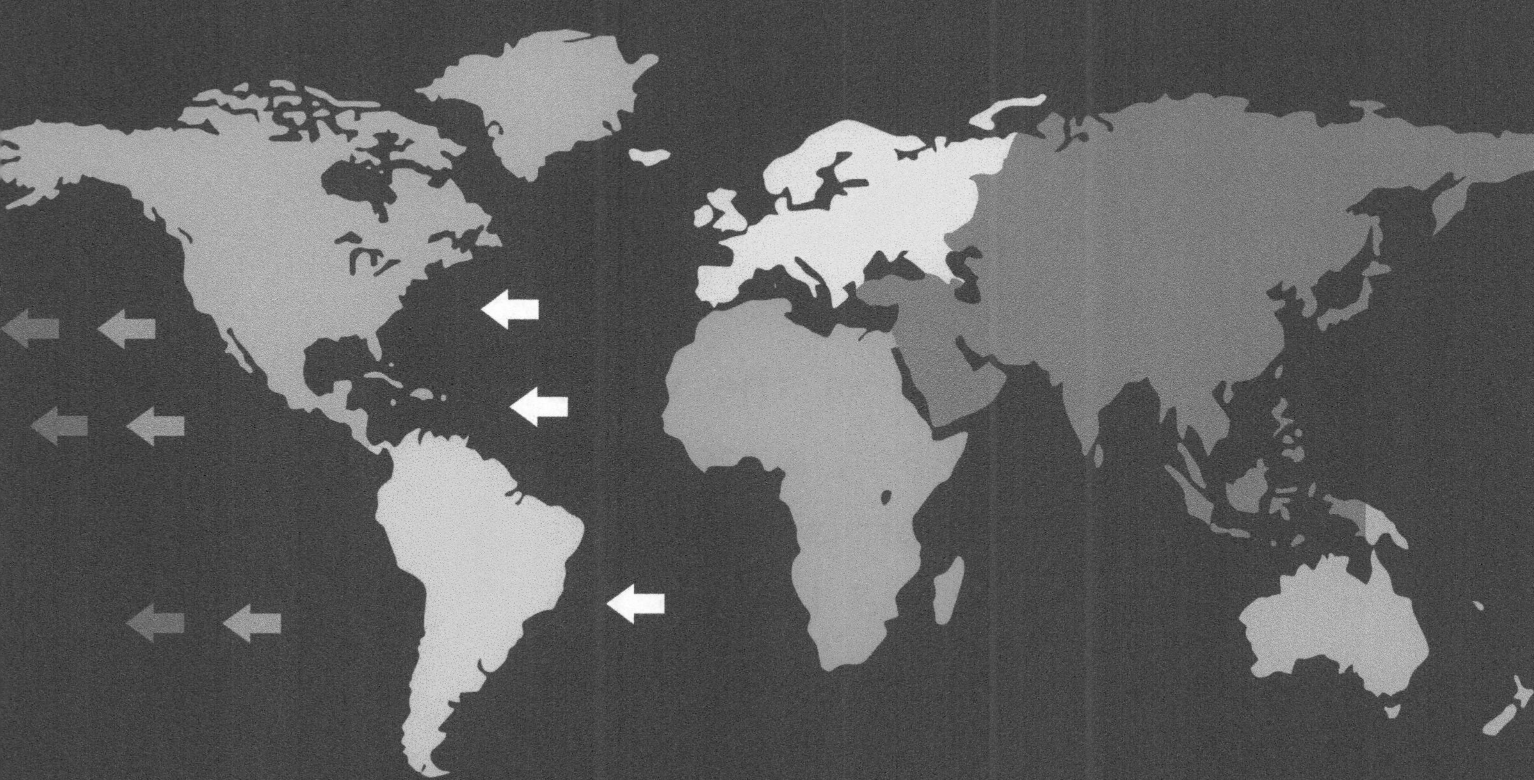

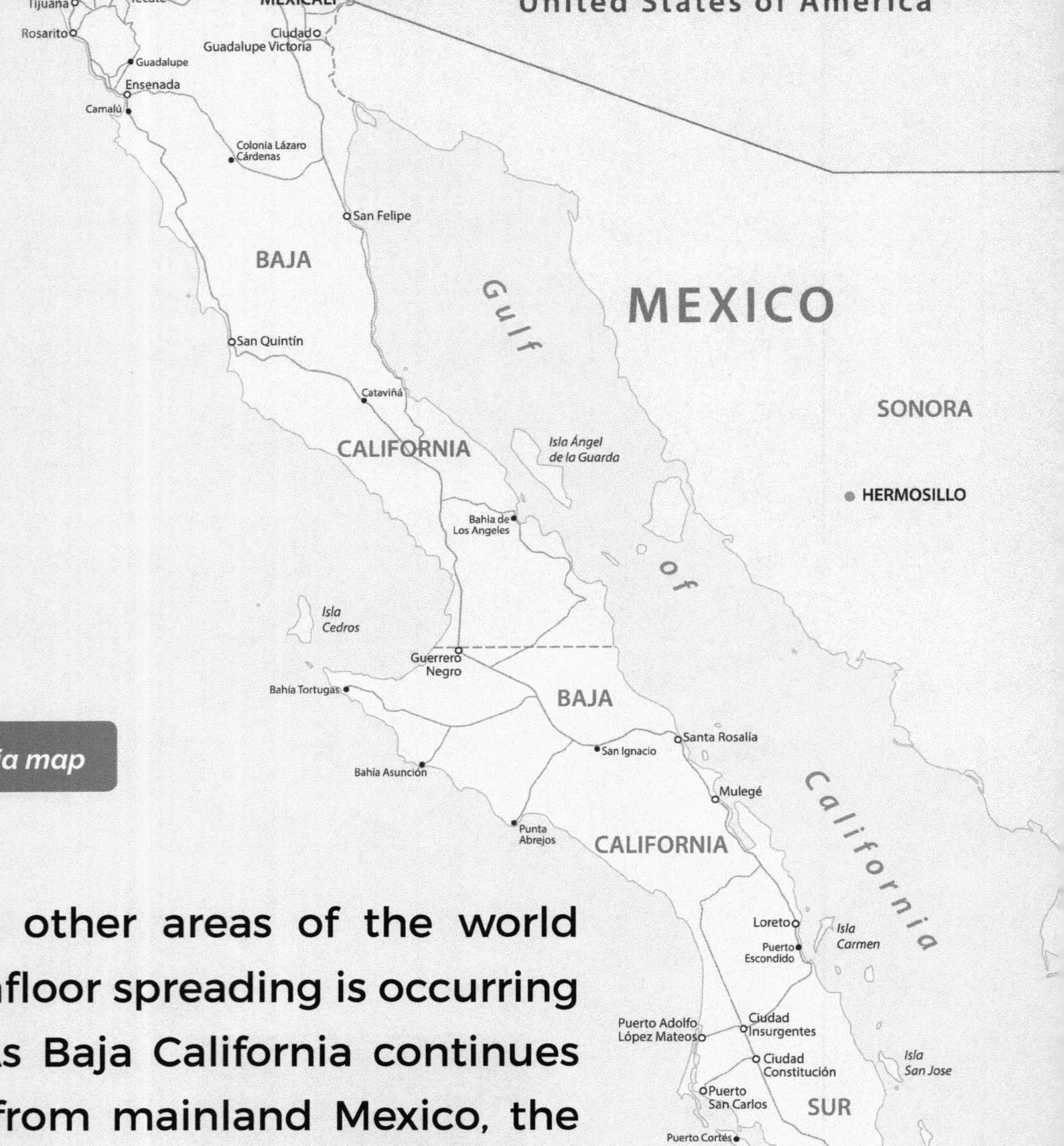

Baja California map

There are other areas of the world where seafloor spreading is occurring as well. As Baja California continues to move from mainland Mexico, the seafloor is spreading and the ocean water flows in.

Manmade interference can sometimes cause minor earthquakes as well. For example, explosions from dynamite or atomic events can cause earthquakes.

Dynamite blast on a mining site

Water pressure can also cause earthquakes. If liquid wastes are injected deep underground or pressure results from retaining too much water in dam reservoirs, the resulting displaced energy can cause earthquakes.

Water flowing through a damaged dam.

HOW ARE EARTHQUAKES MEASURED?

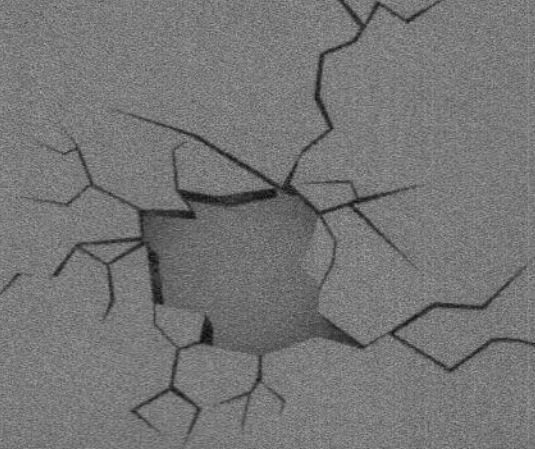

A special piece of equipment called a seismograph displays the waves that an earthquake causes.

Seismograph

The sensors in a seismograph are electromagnetic and can translate the motion of the ground into electrical pulses. The instrument shows the pattern of the strength and duration of the waves with a graph.

Seismological device for measuring earthquakes

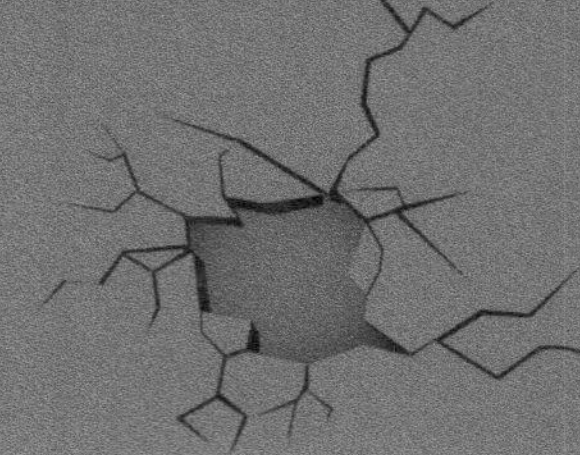

The most common scale used to record the size and force of an earthquake is the Richter scale.

How the Richter Magnitude Scale of Earthquakes is determined from a seismograph.

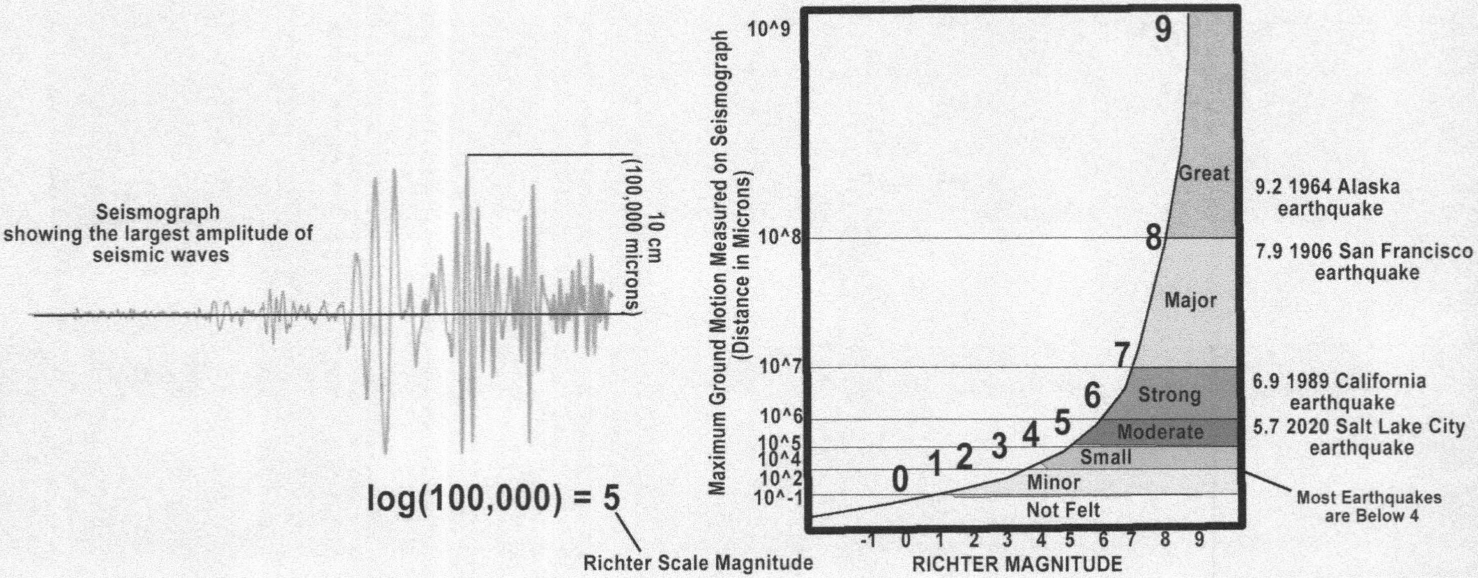

Seismograph
showing the largest amplitude of
seismic waves

10 cm
(100,000 microns)

log(100,000) = 5

Richter Scale Magnitude

Maximum Ground Motion Measured on Seismograph
(Distance in Microns)

10^9
10^8
10^7
10^6
10^5
10^4
10^2
10^-1

0 1 2 3 4 5 6 7 8 9

Great
Major
Strong
Moderate
Small
Minor
Not Felt

-1 0 1 2 3 4 5 6 7 8 9
RICHTER MAGNITUDE

9.2 1964 Alaska earthquake
7.9 1906 San Francisco earthquake
6.9 1989 California earthquake
5.7 2020 Salt Lake City earthquake
Most Earthquakes are Below 4

This scale, created by Charles Richter, measures the power of an earthquake using a number from 0 to 10 from a seismograph reading.

Charles Richter

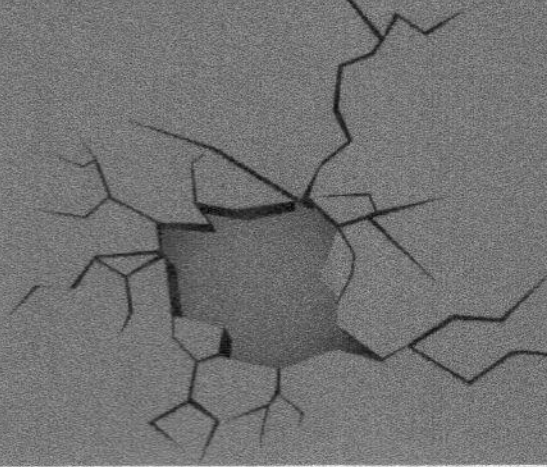

However, these measurements are not the easiest to interpret because they use a logarithmic scale. An earthquake that measures 2 instead of 1 isn't twice as powerful than the 1, it is 10 times more powerful!

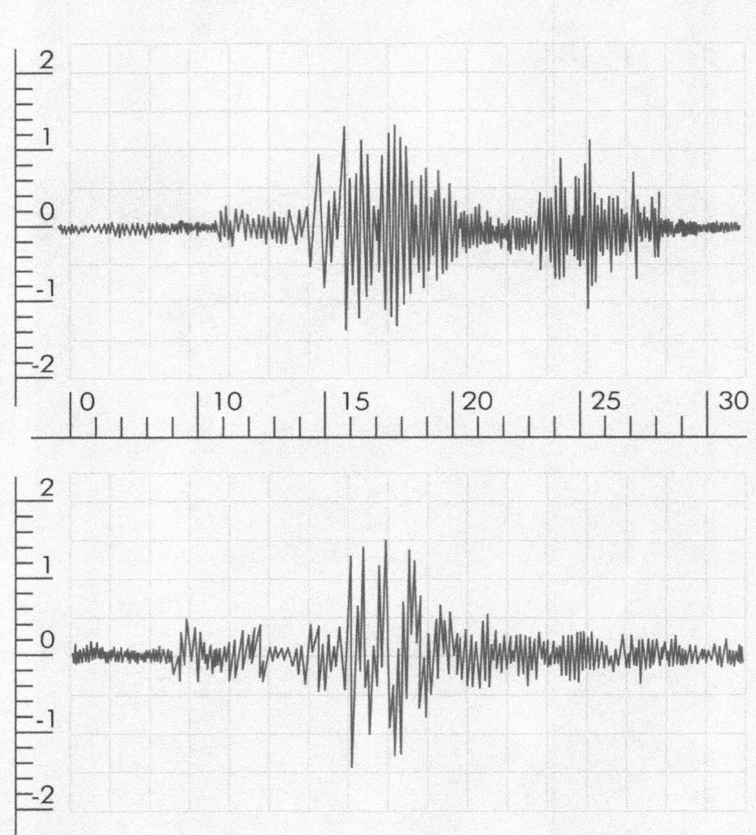

An illustration of a graph output by a seismograph

As each whole number increases it also means that 32 times more energy is omitted. There are over 900,000 tiny earthquakes every year that a seismograph can measure, but people don't feel.

Over 900,000 tiny earthquakes happen every year.

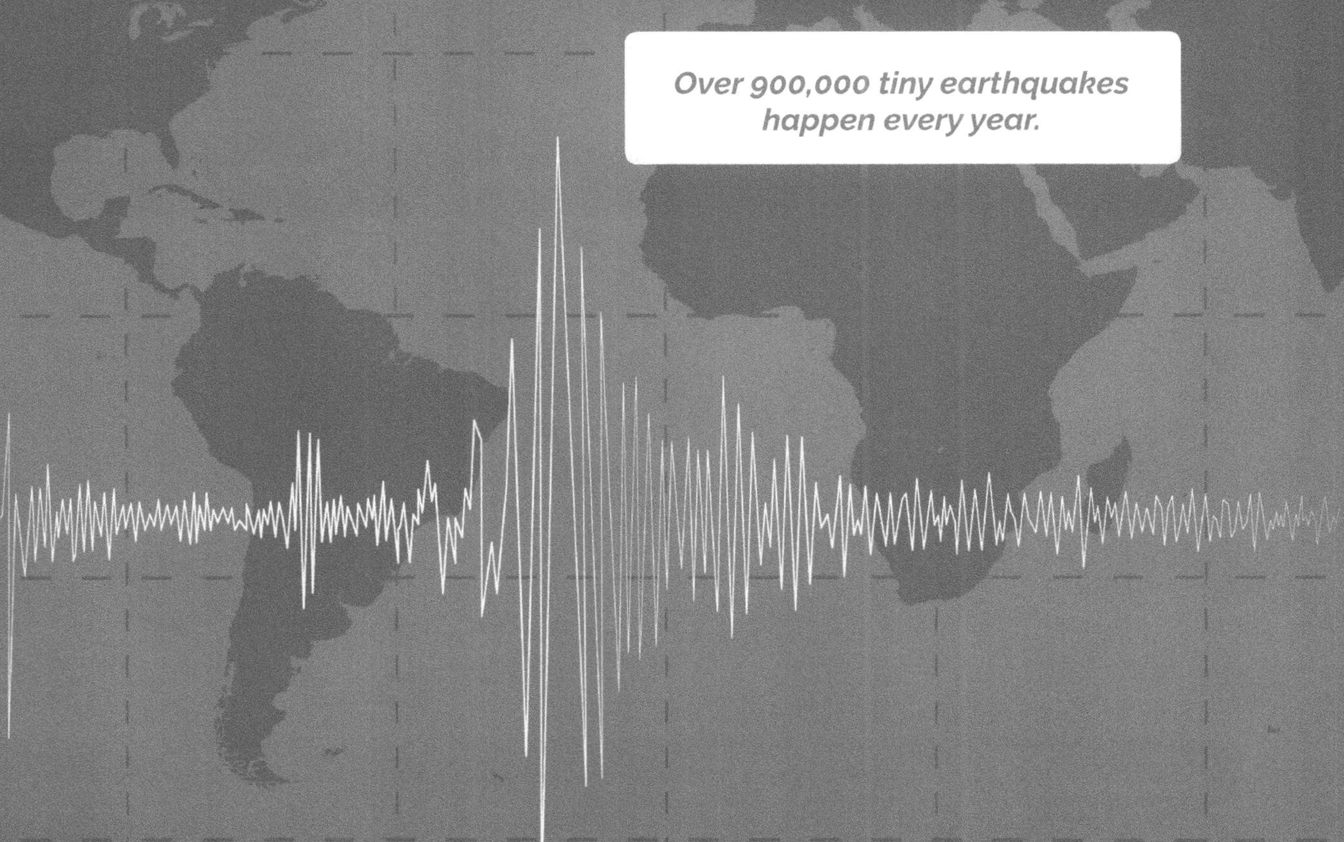

There are another 30,000 or so that range from 2.5 to 5.5 on the Richter Scale. Generally, these only cause minor damage although people do feel them. Once you get to 6 and above, there are fewer earthquakes that register in this range.

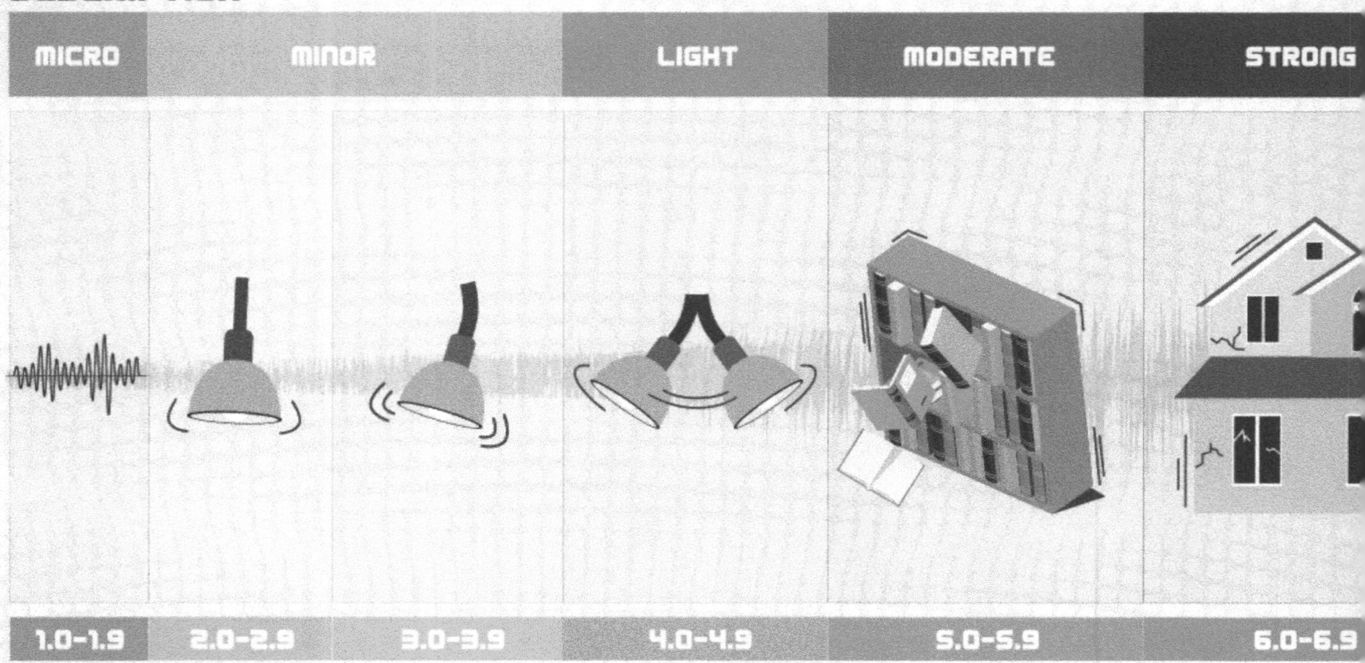

A strong earthquake would be a 6 to 6.9 and a major earthquake would range from 7 to 7.0. Luckily, earthquakes measuring 8 and above don't happen very often, usually only once in every 5 to 10 years..

Richter Earthquake Magnitude Scale and Classes

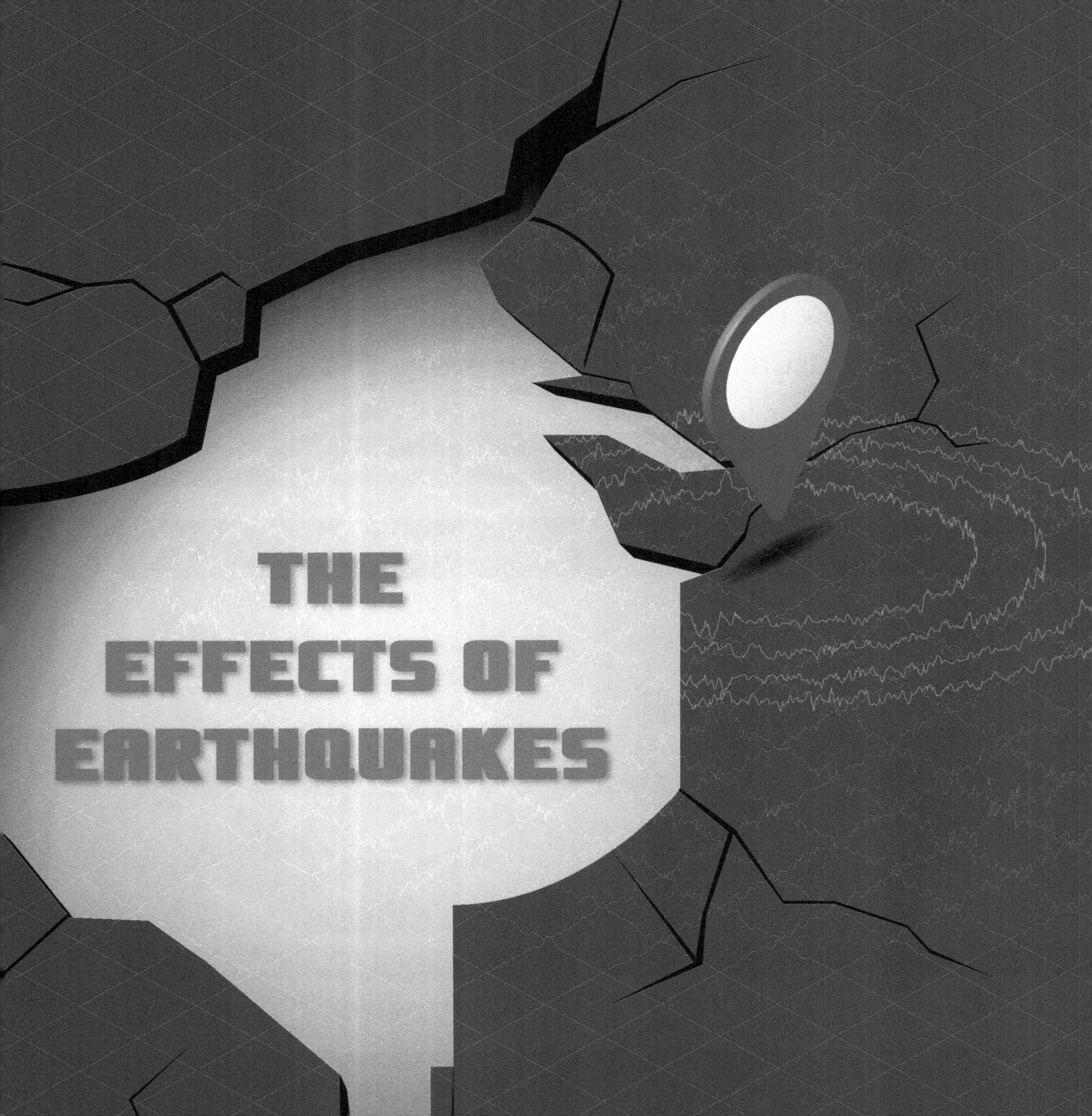
THE
EFFECTS OF
EARTHQUAKES

Strong earthquakes change the surface of the Earth. In addition to the effects of the ground shaking, earthquakes can alter the flow of groundwater and cause landslides as well as mudflows.

Mud flow from a volcano eruption

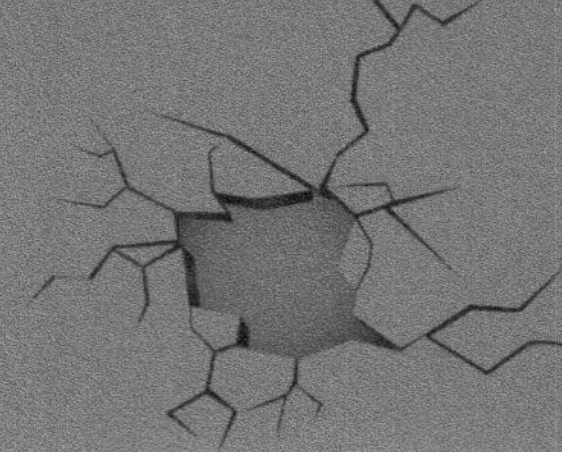

They also bring down buildings, bridges, and dams.

Collapsed building, bridges, house and dam due to earthquake

When an earthquake is this powerful, many people die as well when they get trapped inside buildings or are traveling over bridges. Another devastating effect of earthquakes is a tsunami.

An aerial view of damage to Ōtsuchi, Japan, a week after a 9.0 magnitude earthquake, 2011

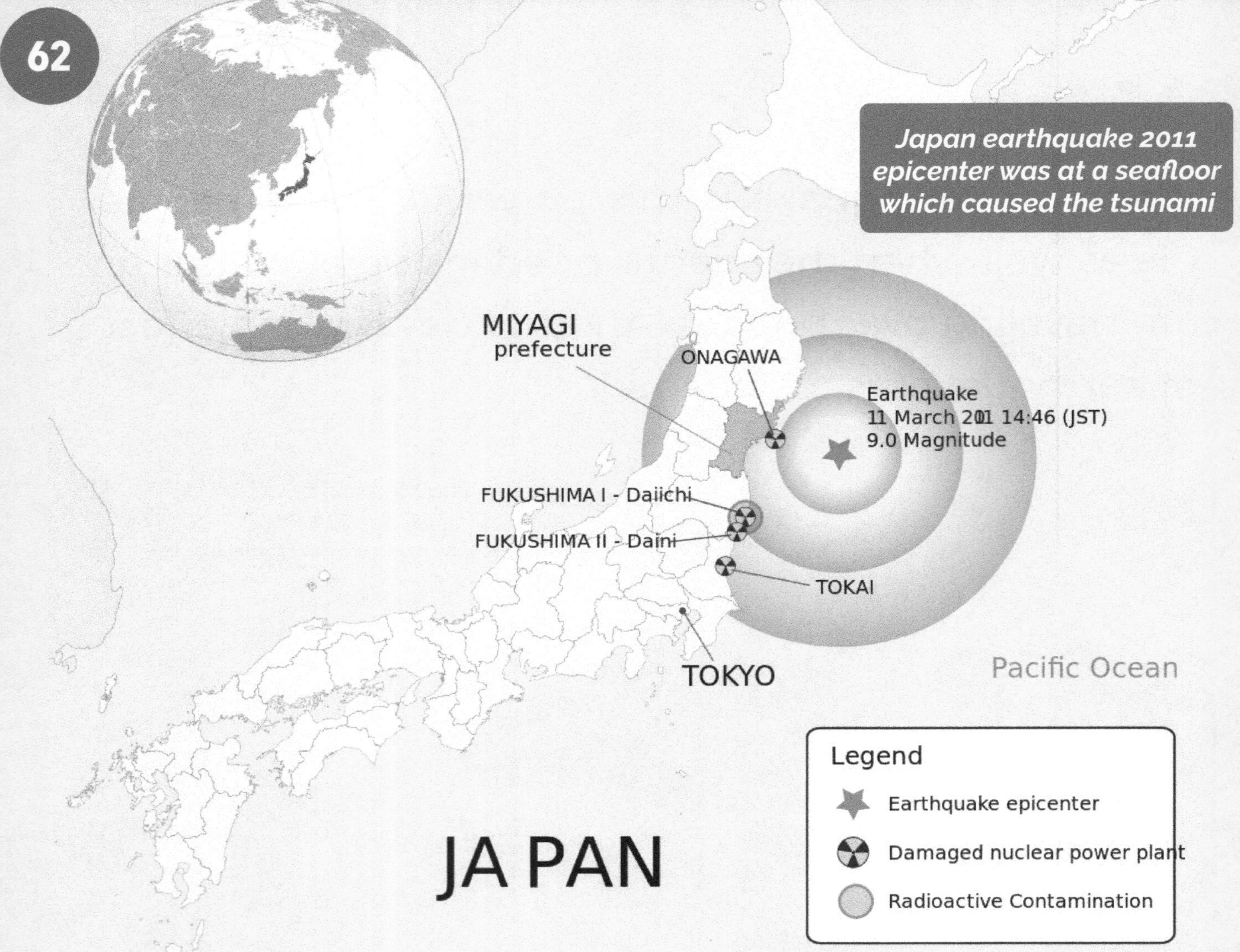

If the epicenter of a powerful earthquake is on the seafloor, the waves spread out and begin to travel as fast as 800 kilometers per hour.

Once the tsunami hits the shore it might be as tall as 30 meters high. It's so powerful that it can wipe out cities in a few minutes.

An aerial view of damage in Japan after a tsunami.

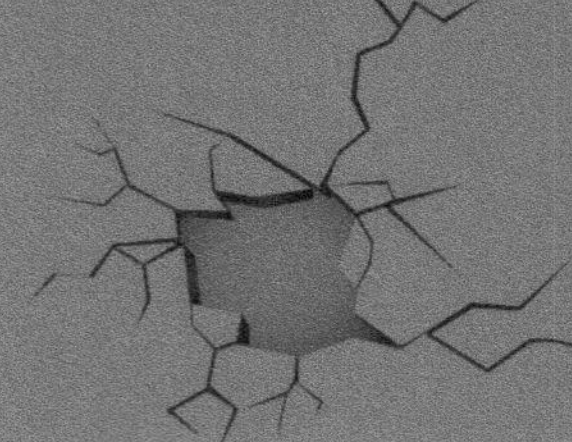

Yet another devastating consequence of earthquakes are the fires that result from gas lines, power lines, and other sources.

Massive explosion in a chemical plant in Texas

In 1906, a major portion of the city of San Francisco burned uncontrollably over a period of three days.

Aftermath of San Francisco earthquake, 1906

In 1923, a huge fire happened after an earthquake in Tokyo and it caused tremendous damage over a wide area.

An image of destruction of Ginza area in Tokyo from the 1923 Great Kantō earthquake

SUMMARY

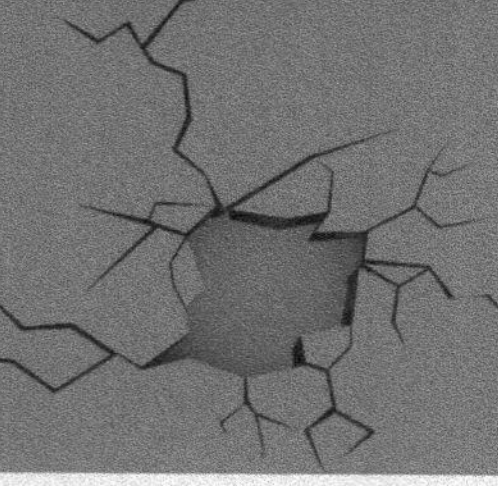

SHAKES AND QUAKES

Natural Disasters that Change the Earth

The theory of tectonic plates has only been widely accepted since the 1950s. Earthquakes are caused by the movements of these plates at the ruptured sections of the Earth's crust called faults. The tectonic plates are constantly moving in very small increments so we don't usually feel their movement unless there is a sizable earthquake. However, very powerful earthquakes cause widespread destruction and change the Earth's surface. At least one catastrophic earthquake happens somewhere around the world once every 5 to 10 years. The Richter scale is a logarithmic scale that is used to measure earthquakes.

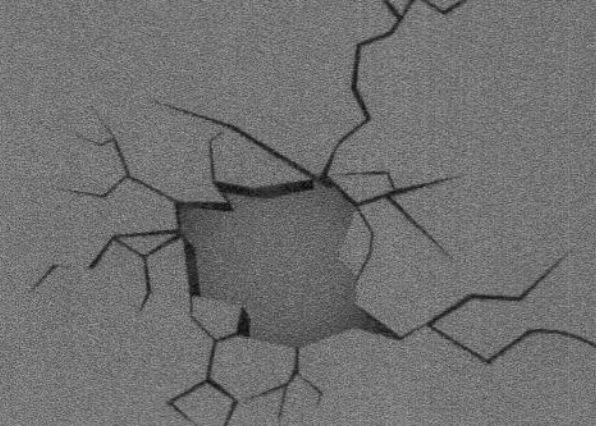

Awesome! Now that you've learned about earthquakes and their causes, you may want to read more about tectonic plates in the Baby Professor Book, **Why Do Tectonic Plates Crash and Slip? Geology Book for Kids | Children's Earth Sciences Books Baby Professor.**

Visit

www.speedypublishing.com
to download Free Baby Professor eBooks and view our catalog of new and exciting Children's Books

Lightning Source UK Ltd.
Milton Keynes UK
UKHW051330040121
376379UK00002B/113